Citizenship

Philip Steele

Evans

EVANS BROTHERS LIMITED

Published by
Evans Brothers Limited
2A Portman Mansions
Chiltern Street
London W1M ILE

© Evans Brothers Limited 2001

First published in 2001

Printed in Dubai

British Library Cataloguing in Publication Data
Steele, Philip
    Citizenship
    1. Citizenship - Juvenile literature
    I. Title
    323.6

ISBN 0237520478

Editor: Nicola Barber
Consultant: Janet Edwards, Citizenship
            Education Consultant
Design: Simon Borrough
Production: Jenny Mulvanny

Acknowledgements
For permission to reproduce copyright pictorial material, the author and publishers gratefully acknowledge the following:

cover:	(from left) Collections/Roger Scruton
	Collections/Image Ireland/Mark O'Sullivan
	Collections/Liba Taylor
	Collections/Paul Bryans
	Collections/Roger Scruton
	Collections/Anthea Sieveking
page 6:	gettyone stone/Bob Thomas
page 8:	Topham Picturepoint
page 13:	gettyone Stone
page 14:	Topham Picturepoint
page 18:	(from left) Collections/Brian Shuel
	Collections/Anthea Sieveking
	Collections/Liba Taylor
	Collections/Roger Scruton
page 19:	(from left) Collections/Image Ireland/Mark O'Sullivan
	Collections/Liba Taylor
	Collections/Roger Scruton
	Collections/Paul Bryans
page 20:	Collections/Nigel Hawkins
page 22:	Rex Features/Tim Rooke
page 24:	Rex Features
page 27:	gettyone Stone/Jon Riley
page 29:	Topham Picturepoint
page 31:	Rex Features
page 32:	Collections/Michael St Maur Sheil
page 34:	Collections
page 36:	Magnum
page 39:	Rex Features
page 41:	Rex Features/Markus Zeffler
page 43:	Collections/Brian Shuel
page 45:	Topham Picturepoint
page 47:	Rex Features
page 50:	Rex Features/David Hartley
page 55:	Collections/Paul Bryans
page 56:	Rex Features
page 58:	Magnum
page 60:	Collections/Liz Stares
page 62:	gettyone Stone
page 63:	Collections/Nigel French
page 64:	Magnum/C. Steele-Perkins
page 65:	Topham/Tony Savino
page 66:	Magnum /C. Steele-Perkins
page 68:	Magnum
page 70:	Rex Features/Dennis Cameron
page 72:	Collections/John Callan
page 73:	Robert Harding
page 75:	Collections/Keith Pritchard
page 77:	Topham Picturepoint

When do we need to fit in with the crowd and when do we need to stand up for ourselves?

You are a unique individual, different from anyone else in the world. You share the world with almost six billion other individuals. This book is about how you connect with them.

Some of those individuals you know very well. You share your life with them from day to day. They are your parents or guardians, your grandparents, brothers or sisters. They are your neighbours and close friends. Others you don't know quite so well. They may go to the same school or live in the same town or village. You may buy your food from them or ride in buses driven by them. Their lives cross paths with yours from time to time. Still others who live in the same country as you lead lives very different from those of the people in your neighbourhood.

Most of the people in the world don't know you and you don't know them. Many of them live far away. They speak different languages and may at first seem to lead very different lives from yours. Even so, if you were to meet them, or exchange letters or e-mail, you might find that you have a surprising amount in common with many of them, as human beings.

Making connections

All these people belong to many different, overlapping groups. They can be divided up according to their age or their sex, their family relationships, their religious beliefs or ethnic groups, the language they speak or the work they do. Together they make up the complicated network that we call society. Society changes all the time. For example, modern technology and medicine are rapidly changing the way that we live.

We all depend on other individuals in society and some of them depend on us. A baby may depend on parents for food and care when it is born, but when those parents have become old, it is they who will need looking after.

An organised world

Societies have to organise themselves if their individual members are to survive and thrive. In a well-organised society, laws are drawn up to prevent people from harming others and to protect the weak. There are hospitals for the sick, schools for children, and houses to live in. There are roads for travelling and supplies of food so that people do not starve. The ways in which societies are organised and governed are called political systems. These systems have varied greatly over the ages. The nature of political systems is shaped by economic forces – by the way in which people work and are rewarded, and by who holds power or owns land.

Citizens and citizenship

The word 'citizen' originally meant somebody who lived in a city. Today the word is used to describe someone who belongs to a particular state or nation. For example, when you apply for a passport, you might be asked: 'Are you a British citizen?'. The term is also used in a much more general sense than this, to describe an individual in relation to society as a whole. We might ask, for example: 'Should citizens be free to follow their own religious beliefs?'.

The relationship between a citizen and society is governed by formal and informal agreements. A citizen is generally allowed certain personal rights within society. Examples might include equal treatment with other citizens, the protection of the law or the freedom to communicate with others. These are called civil rights. In return, individuals are normally expected to respect the rights of others and to play their part in making society work for the good of all. For example they might be expected to obey the law, pay their taxes or vote in a general election.

There are many areas of contact between the individual citizen and social organisations. There is government and politics. There is work, economics and social welfare. There is justice and the law. There are public services and voluntary organisations. Many of these areas overlap. They all affect us as individuals. Social organisation takes place at many levels – within the home, in villages and cities, within regions and nations. It extends far beyond national borders, too. Today we could all describe

7

ourselves as citizens of the world, for we are all linked by communications, by economics, by law and by international organisations such as the European Union (EU) or the United Nations (UN).

The way in which an individual fits into this complicated social jigsaw puzzle, either by choice or necessity, is called citizenship. People sometimes say that somebody is a 'good' citizen. But what is meant by good or bad citizenship? Ask any group of people and you will probably be given a different answer. Some people might see the aim of citizenship as getting the individual to fit in, so that society functions more smoothly. Others might argue that a good citizen is someone who tries to make society operate more fairly. So, good citizenship could mean doing as you are told – but it could just as well mean the opposite!

Conduct a survey: ask people of different ages what they think it means to be a good citizen. Ask them to name a local person who they would nominate for the Good Citizen award in your area.

A political system in which people can vote representatives into government is called a democracy. Effective citizenship and a fair and just democracy are two sides of the same coin. If citizens like an existing political system, they can support it and help to make it work. If they don't like it, they can challenge it and work to change it. These are their rights as citizens.

Elections should offer us a chance to decide how we are governed. Are they effective?

THE NORTHERN IRELAND ELECTION · THURSDAY 30 MAY

YOUR VOICE. YOUR CHOICE. YOUR FUTURE

ISSUED BY THE NORTHERN IRELAND OFFICE

VOTE X FOR ONE PARTY. POLLS OPEN 7 AM TO 10 PM.

When might it be moral to refuse to do what you are told?
Give an example from the past of a protest that changed society for the good. Give an example from the current news of a controversial issue about which some people are protesting.

What types of behaviour do you think are acceptable when challenging authority?
Is it ever right to break the law?

It is in the interest of all citizens to understand how society functions. They should find out what is going on in the world, asking questions and debating issues. They should find out how political and economic systems work – and how they affect everyone in society, not just them.

Most people would agree that both citizens and governments have a duty to behave morally. This means that individuals and groups in society should treat others in a way that they would like to be treated themselves. They should think about the welfare of society as a whole as well as about themselves and their own interests.

Choose a country that is in the news at the moment.
For the country of your choice find out:
• the total population
• the type of government
• the language(s) spoken
• the religions practised
• the main products
• the background to a topical issue featured in the news.

The annual Notting Hill carnival in London brings the community together to have fun.

Good citizens should not cut themselves off from others, but take part in the life of the community. Citizenship is about finding the right balance between being an individual and being a member of society.

In groups, make a list of ways in which adult citizens take part in the life of the community. How can young people take part? (Think of both formal and informal ways.)

T he world is divided into countries, or nations. These are not natural areas that have always existed. They are regions of government, created and organised by human beings, and their boundaries may change over the years. Small countries sometimes join together to form bigger ones, or big countries break up into smaller ones. Today, there are over 190 independent (self-governing) nations in the world, as well as many other special territories and dependencies (lands that are ruled by another country).

National borders may be natural frontiers, such as mountains, coastlines or rivers. They may also be completely artificial divides, drawn across the map as a result of past political problems or wars, or of international treaties. National borders may pass right through the traditional homeland of a people, forcing members of one group that speak the same language and follow the same way of life to become citizens of two or more different countries.

Use an atlas to find an example of a national boundary that follows:
- a river
- a mountain range
- a sea coast
- a lake shore
- a line of latitude.

Find examples of boundaries that do not seem to follow any natural feature. Can you find out why these boundaries have been drawn in this way?

People settling in a new land must normally apply to be citizens of that country and agree to obey its laws. Wars, oppression or poverty may make citizens flee from their home country. They are often forced to seek asylum or refuge in another land. They become refugees.

National nuts and bolts

Nations may be structured in all sorts of different ways. They are like frameworks, bolted together in response to political events, economic forces and ethnic and cultural groupings. They can hold people together – or set them apart.

Let's look at the nuts and bolts of where we live in northwest Europe. The British Isles is a group of islands lying in shallow waters off the northwestern coast of Europe. The biggest island is called Great Britain, and the second biggest is Ireland. The British Isles are divided into two independent nations: the United Kingdom of Great Britain and Northern Ireland (UK), and the Republic of Ireland. The UK is a political union of three smaller countries called England, Scotland and Wales, together with the province of Northern Ireland. The UK also has very close links with various small, self-governing islands. These include the Isle of Man, and the Channel Islands of Jersey and Guernsey.

At times during their history, the British Isles have been divided up into many small kingdoms. Today they are recognised internationally as two independent nations.

What are the capital cities of the
United Kingdom, England, Scotland,
Wales and Northern Ireland?

*Dublin, on the River
Liffey, is the capital of
the Republic of Ireland.
It is also its biggest
city and its centre of
government. Why might
more people live in a
capital city than in
a country town?*

What is the current situation in the Northern Ireland peace process? Cut out items from newspapers and magazines to illustrate the political situation.

The independent Republic of Ireland occupies most of Ireland, apart from a region in the northeast which forms the UK province of Northern Ireland. Some of the people in Northern Ireland want that province to become part of the Republic. Others want it to remain in the UK. This has led to many years of violent conflict. The political parties in Northern Ireland and the governments of the UK and the Irish Republic are trying to agree a peace settlement. Disputes such as this are common in many parts of the world.

Now let's look at the way nations are bolted together on the inside. Many are divided into regions, which may be called various names. Some nations are centralised, which means that they have a single, central government and one set of laws for the whole country. The Irish Republic is an example of a centralised state. Other countries, such as Germany or the United States, are organised on federal lines. That means that each region can pass its own laws and raise its own taxes, within a framework of national government.

Do you live in the United Kingdom? Do you think that the region or country where you live should have more independence from Westminster? What additional powers, over and above those currently held by local government or by the Scottish Parliament, or the Welsh or Northern Irish assemblies, do you think your region or country would benefit from having:
- defence?
- road building?
- school inspection?
- VAT levels?

Invite a locally elected politician to your school to discuss these questions. If you live in the Irish Republic, do you think that power could be devolved in the provinces?

The structure of the UK lies somewhere between a centralised and a federal system. It has a strong central government, but since 1998 it has devolved, or handed over, varying amounts of power to a directly elected Scottish Parliament and a Welsh Assembly. Some people argue that similar power should be extended to the regions of England.

This board shows how the public voted to authorise the setting up of a Welsh Assembly in 1998. What percentage of the public voted? Was it a close result? In what way is this board different from one showing the result of an English or Scottish election?

Give an example of a country whose regions are referred to as:

- states
- lands
- cantons
- provinces
- departments
- territories
- counties.

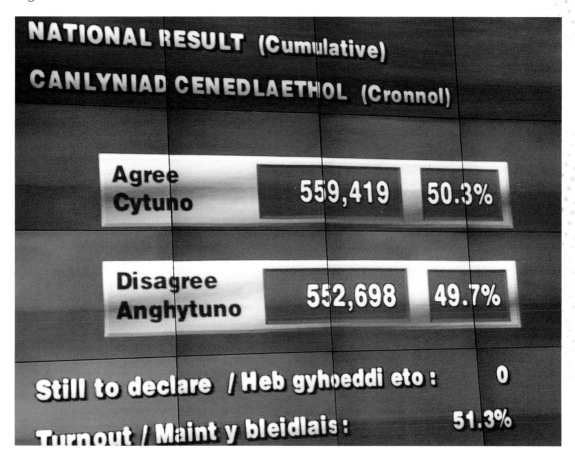

NATIONAL RESULT (Cumulative)

CANLYNIAD CENEDLAETHOL (Cronnol)

Agree Cytuno	559,419	50.3%
Disagree Anghytuno	552,698	49.7%

Still to declare / Heb gyhoeddi eto : 0

Turnout / Maint y bleidlais : 51.3%

All parts of the United Kingdom, and the Irish Republic too, are subdivided into small administrative regions called counties or unitary authorities. Administration at this level is called local government. Elected local councils exist at the level of city, county, town or village. They may deal with such matters as planning, housing, refuse collection and local services. They may also run schools, public libraries or hospitals. They set levels of local taxation to pay for locally run services.

Population and statistics

Countries are, of course, more than organisations and structures. The word nation is often used to describe not so much the political structure of a country as all the people who live there. A democratic national framework should reflect the wishes of the majority of the citizens it contains – its population.

In order to run a country effectively, information has to be gathered about the people who live in it. Most countries count their population in a census every ten years or so. For the years in between, they have to estimate whether that figure has got bigger or smaller. All kinds of other useful facts or statistics can be collected. These may sound a bit boring when they are in a long list, but until we know the facts, we cannot understand the nature of the society we live in and pinpoint its problems. Statistics are useless until they are acted upon or applied so that they do some good for people.

The following are some useful facts that were gathered about the United Kingdom in 2000. Can you think of ways in which these statistics might be made use of, so that people can plan for the future?

- The total UK population in 2000 was estimated at 59.8 million.

- It was growing very slowly, at a rate of just 0.1% each year.

- UK males can expect to live to the age of 74 and females to the age of 80.

- 19% of the population is under 15 years of age. 16% is over 65 years of age.

- 89% of the UK population lives in cities or in towns (settlements of over 2000 people).

- 99% of adults in the UK can read and write.

Statistics make more sense when you compare them with those of other countries. Can you find out the above figures for the following countries?

Argentina (South America)
Canada (North America)
Chad (Africa)
Costa Rica (Central America)
Fiji (Oceania)
France (Europe)
India (Asia)
Republic of Ireland (Europe)
Japan (Asia)
Portugal (Europe)
Russian Federation (Europe/Asia)
Australia (Oceania)

Most countries are made up of citizens of various peoples or ethnic groups, speaking a variety of languages, and following different religious beliefs or ways of life. The largest ethnic groups are known as majorities and smaller ones as minorities.

The population of the British Isles is made up of many different ethnic groups. The mixture of peoples has been changing constantly over the last 2000 years.

Many different ethnic groups live in the British Isles. Some of these mixed together long ago, when peoples such as Angles, Saxons, Vikings and Normans invaded the islands from mainland Europe. Celtic peoples are descended from some of the earliest peoples of the British Isles. They include the Welsh, Scots, Irish, Cornish and Manx. The largest ethnic group in the UK is formed by the English, who are closely related to Germanic peoples such as the Dutch and the Germans.

Nationality means different things to different people. What does it mean to you? Is it best indicated by which football team you support? Is it something you don't really think about until you travel abroad?

Other peoples have settled in the British Isles, too – Roma (often known as Gypsies), Flemings, French, Jews and peoples from Central and Eastern Europe. Many British people are descended from families who originally came from more distant parts of the world that were once ruled by the United Kingdom – Greek Cypriots, Turkish Cypriots, Indians, Pakistanis, Bangladeshis, Hong Kong Chinese, African-Caribbeans, Ugandans and Nigerians.

Many of these people have brought their own languages to the British Isles. English is the common language and is spoken throughout Great Britain and Ireland. English has spread around the world, too, and in 1999 was spoken as a first language by 322 million people worldwide. That makes it the third most spoken language in the world after Chinese and Spanish.

Welsh is spoken by half a million people in Wales, where it is often used in everyday life, in schools and on television and radio. So too is Gaelic, which may be heard in the Highlands and Islands of Scotland. In the Lowlands and Borders, the unique accents and words of Scots may be heard. The Irish language is still widely spoken in some regions of Ireland.

A person from the UK might describe themselves as European, or as British – or as Scottish, Irish, Welsh, English – or perhaps as Jewish, Jamaican or Bangladeshi. They might use a more local term, saying they are a Yorkshire man or woman (from one of the English counties), a 'Geordie' (from the northeastern region of England) or a 'Brummie' (from the city of Birmingham).

How would you describe your nationality? Ask this question of family and friends and discuss your findings.

Any country which has such a rich mixture of ways of life, languages and dialects is lucky in many ways. Ideas and energy tend to grow from contact between different worlds, not from isolation. Sections of society that choose to remain ignorant about the way in which other people live lose touch with the real world. Fear, hatred and bigotry grow from ignorance.

Many people choose to identify themselves by their religion. "I am a British Hindu," they might explain, or "He is a Northern Ireland Protestant." In many countries, religion is closely tied to the idea of the nation. Some nations include a religion in their official name, such as the Islamic Republic of Iran. In others, such as the United States, the nation officially stands back from any one religion, leaving faith as a matter of individual choice and treating all religions equally.

Within the United Kingdom, the policy varies. Wales has no established, or official church. In England, however, the Church of England is established and part of the political framework. The Church of Scotland is also established, but is part of a different religious tradition – Christians would describe it as Presbyterian rather than Episcopalian.

Take an opinion poll amongst members of your school class.

• Should there be nationally established religions, or is faith something that should be kept at a purely personal level?

• Should people of a particular religious background be allowed to have their own schools, or should children of all faiths be educated together?

• Should religious studies be a compulsory subject in all schools? In the UK it is a compulsory subject, while in the USA it is against the law in state schools to teach religious studies.

The Swaminarayan Hindu Mission in Neasden, northwest London. Religious beliefs have always played an important part in the history of the British Isles.

Christians make up the greatest section of the UK population, but there are also many Muslims, Hindus, Sikhs and Jews. Many British people do not attend any form of worship on a regular basis. Many are atheists, some are agnostic and others are humanists.

Running up the flag

Flags are badges or emblems, and every nation in the world has one. They flutter from flagpoles and can serve a useful purpose – in identifying a ship at sea, for example. In some schools in the USA, you would have to start each day by saluting the national flag. In many countries flags are treated with extreme respect, because they are seen to be a symbol of the nation. They are flown on public buildings and on private homes, too. However in some other countries, including the UK, flags are not considered to be so important and they are flown less often in public places.

Songs can be a symbol of nationhood. They are called national anthems and some of them have stirring tunes. Some have been sung for hundreds of years, which is why they often have rather old-fashioned words that refer to historical events rather than the present day. Even so, when anthems are played before a football or rugby match, the crowd roars along.

Give examples of places and circumstances when flags are flown in the UK.

Imagine you have been given the job of writing words for a new national anthem. You might want to borrow the tune of a song in the charts that you like. What kind of things do you think should be included in your anthem to reflect the way we live today?

It could be argued that symbols like these are useful in uniting a nation, particularly in times of strife or war. But being a good citizen is not really about waving flags or singing the right songs. It is about taking action to benefit and unite, rather than divide, the world's peoples and nations.

My country, right or wrong?

To be a good citizen, do you have to love and respect your nation? Ask people anywhere what they admire or like about the country in which they live, and they may mention anything from its music to its food, the friendliness of its people, its way of life or even its climate.

People often feel proud of the country where they live because of its traditions and customs, or its artistic, scientific and sporting achievements. Some people enjoy the feeling of belonging to a group, of a shared background. In a world where more and more things are the same, it is good to see traditional festivals still taking place or people still wearing the beautiful costumes of their own region.

A love of one's country may include respect for the past generations who made today's way of life possible. National days may celebrate a country's hard-won freedoms or its struggle for independence. By discovering the history of their country, people

Each year, on 11 November, a ceremony is held at the Cenotaph memorial in Whitehall, London. It commemorates those who fought and died for their country in the First World War (1914-18) and the Second World War (1939-45).

can sometimes gain a better understanding about its place in the modern world. However, Dr Samuel Johnson, one of the best-known English writers of the 1700s, was far from enthusiastic about patriotism, or love of one's country. He described it as 'the last refuge of a scoundrel'. What did he mean? He was probably thinking of people who stir up national feelings in order to create trouble or further their own political ambition. Unthinking or aggressive patriotism is sometimes referred to as jingoism.

Once people begin to believe that their own country is better than any other, or that their own people are superior to another, it may lead to racism. This sets one group of human beings against another. Because we all depend on each other, anything that divides the human race as a whole also weakens the nation.

Are we entitled to criticise our country when we see it following a path we think is wrong? We may love a child, but we still tell him off when he does something wrong. Does a country have the right to deserve our love when it demands it? Truly patriotic values surely include both good citizenship and good government as a *two-way* process.

Should we place limits on 'loving' one's country? Should we support our country at all times, whether it is in the right or in the wrong? Should we be expected to fight in a war and die for our country? Does that depend on whether we as individuals believe that war to be just? Can somebody who refuses to fight out of respect for all human life be just as patriotic as someone who fights? Discuss in a group.

Some people argue that every right carries a relevant responsibility. For each of the following rights name a corresponding responsibility:
- the right to free speech
- the right to receive the protection of the law
- the right to free education
- the right to fair treatment.

A page from the Amazon.com website. The internet has broken down international borders and changed the way people do business.

Nations cannot isolate themselves from the rest of the world. People have always moved from one part of the world to another. Business and trade are international – there may be Japanese-owned factories in France and French-owned factories in Japan. So, many people around the world share problems and have common aims.

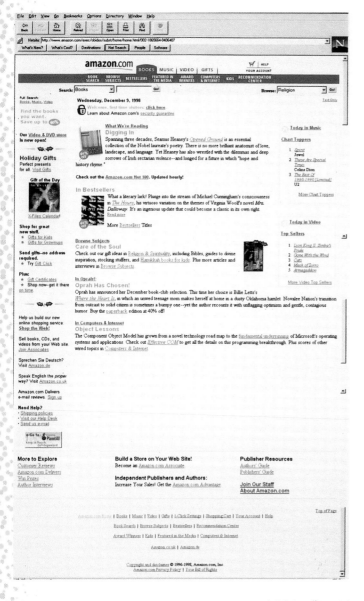

Travel between countries is easier than ever. Modern ways of communicating, such as telephones, faxes, e-mail, radio or satellite television are fast and ignore national borders. That is what people mean when they say that the world has 'shrunk', or that we now live in a 'global village'. Because of these changes, many independent nation states are in the process of change. They have lost much of the power and influence they had 100 years ago. They are working increasingly on an international level.

Countries have always made treaties or agreements with other countries. In the last 50 years most nations have extended the nuts and bolts of their national structure by joining up with other regional or international bodies. The aims of these may be economic, political, legal or military. They may provide opportunities for discussing matters of shared interest, such as peace and security within a region, movement of people, provision of work, standards of living, and financial matters such as exchange rates.

International links

The United Kingdom is a member of many international bodies:

The *Commonwealth of Nations* is a worldwide forum for discussion between nations. Most of the members were once part of the British empire, and so have shared trade and political or cultural links for many years.

The *Council of Europe* is an organisation of European nations which aims to promote unity, democracy and human rights.

The *North Atlantic Treaty Organization* (NATO) is a military alliance between the USA and many European nations. It was founded in 1949 in order to defend the USA and its allies from possible attack. In 1999, NATO took on a new role when it invaded the territory of Kosovo, which was ruled by Yugoslavia, with the aim of protecting citizens of Albanian descent from others of Serb descent.

Both the United Kingdom and the Republic of Ireland are members of the *European Union* (EU). This was founded (as the European Economic Community or EEC) in 1957. Current members also include Austria, Belgium, Denmark, France, Finland, Germany, Greece, Italy, Luxembourg, Netherlands, Portugal, Spain and Sweden. Many other European countries are planning to join.

The following are some other important international organisations. Can you find out which countries belong to them and why they were set up? Can you find out how they operate?

- The Arab League (AL)
- Association of Southeast Asian Nations (ASEAN)
- Caribbean Community and Common Market (Caricom)
- Commonwealth of Independent States (CIS)
- World Trade Organization (WTO)
- North American Free Trade Association (NAFTA)
- Organization for Economic Co-operation and Development (OECD)
- Organization of American States (OAS)
- Organization of African Unity (OAU)

Name some Commonwealth countries, members of the Council of Europe, and some members of NATO.

What advantages might a country wishing to join the EU hope to gain by becoming a member? What criteria are used to decide which countries may join?

What are some of the topical issues being debated in the European Parliament? Who is your MEP? What party does he or she represent?

The EU is an economic and political union. It is headed by a Commission based in Brussels, Belgium. The Commission's proposals are carried out by a Council of Ministers from the member states, which is also based in Brussels. Unlike most international organisations, the EU is an extension of the democratic structure of its member states. This means that there is a European Parliament based in Strasbourg, France, which also holds meetings in Luxembourg and Brussels. It has 626 MEPs (Members of the European Parliament) elected directly by the public in each member country every five years. A committee of 222 members represents the regions within the member nations.

How does the European Court of Justice influence citizens of the UK?

Questions of law are considered by a European Court of Justice, based in Luxembourg. It has 15 judges and nine advocates-general taken from member states.

The United Nations

The largest international organisation is the United Nations (UN). Most independent nations – 185 in the year 2000 – belong to the UN. The UN was founded in 1945 as a reaction to the horrors of the Second World War, and it aims to keep peace in the world and to improve human rights and living conditions for all. The UN is headed by a Secretariat. Since 1997, the Secretary-General has been Kofi Annan from the African nation of Ghana. The chief decision-making assembly of the UN is the General Assembly, with delegates from each member state. It is based in New York City, USA.

The most powerful group within the UN is the Security Council. Permanent members include China, the Russian Federation, USA, UK and France. A further five representatives of member states take it in turn to serve on the council. Members have the power of veto (cancelling action with which they disagree). Questions of international law are decided by the 15 judges of the International Court of Justice, based in The Hague, in the Netherlands.

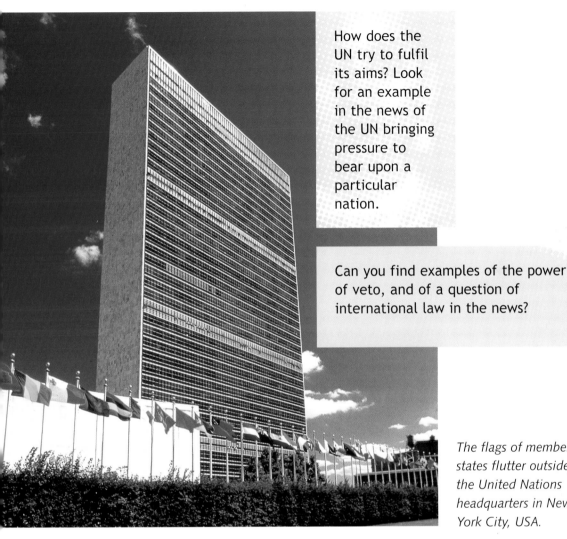

How does the UN try to fulfil its aims? Look for an example in the news of the UN bringing pressure to bear upon a particular nation.

Can you find examples of the power of veto, and of a question of international law in the news?

The flags of member states flutter outside the United Nations headquarters in New York City, USA.

A world government?

The population of the world is growing quickly. By 2025 it may have passed the 8 billion mark, and it could be heading for 12 billion by 2050 if the present growth rate continues. Clearly, such a large number of people need to be organised into units of government of one kind or another. Over the ages the world has been divided into many different types of territories, from vast empires to tiny city states. Could there ever be a world government, divided perhaps into continents and regions?

What would be the difficulties of world government?
What might be its advantages?
Would you hope, one day, to vote in a world government election?

27

In order to carry out its work, the UN has set up specialist agencies, whose activities are funded by the member states. Which of the following areas of action interest you? Can you find out what these UN agencies get up to?

MONEY AND WORK
ILO (International Labour Organization)
IMF (International Monetary Fund)
UNCTAD (Conference on Trade and Development)
UNIDO (Industrial Development Organization)
UNDP (Development Programme)

WORLD FOOD AND FARMING
FAO (Food and Agriculture Organization)
IFAD (International Fund for Agricultural Development)

INTERNATIONAL COMMUNICATIONS
ICAO (International Civil Aviation Organization)
IMO (International Maritime Organization)
ITU (International Telecommunication Union)
UPU (Universal Postal Union)

ENVIRONMENT AND CLIMATE
UNEP (Environment Programme)
UNCED (Conference on Environment and Development, the 'Earth Summit')
WMO (World Meteorological Organization)

CARING FOR PEOPLE
UNCHS (Centre for Human Settlement)
UNESCO (Educational, Scientific and Cultural Organization)
UNHCR (High Commissioner for Refugees)
UNICEF (Children's Fund)
UNIFEM (Development Fund for Women)
WHO (World Health Organization)

5. Economics and Power

hat is the engine that drives society along and decides how we live? It is economics, the way in which we all survive through producing, distributing and consuming food, goods and services. Economics affects every aspect of our lives as individuals and as members of society.

Lessons from history

To understand the economics of the modern world, it helps to know about the past. Ten thousand years ago, people roamed the forests, hunting animals or gathering plants for their supper. But once our ancestors had learned to farm and to live in villages and towns, they started to swap or barter their produce for other goods. Within communities, people began to specialise in certain types of work. Different areas began to specialise in certain types of crop or manufactured item.

This image of ploughing is taken from a medieval manuscript. The economy of the early Middle Ages was based on land and services rather than money and profit.

A thousand years ago in Europe, the economy was based on service and land. This was called the feudal system. The king rewarded nobles who fought for him by giving them land. The poor labourers who worked on this land produced crops for the nobles, who in their turn pledged to protect the labourers. By the 1300s, most people were working for wages. New banks were

founded. These banks lent money even to kings, and soon bankers were collecting so much interest that some became more powerful than the rulers themselves. From the 1500s onwards, European nations began to seize control of lands all over the world. By doing this they obtained raw materials which could be used for making things, and created new markets for selling their goods. They often used slave labour.

During the 1700s and 1800s, many new technologies were developed for manufacturing goods on a large scale. This period was called the Industrial Revolution. Instead of producing goods in small amounts in workshops, people now worked in huge factories. Companies were owned by a few very rich people and controlled by capitalists, people who made a living by buying and selling shares in companies, hoping to make a profit. This form of gambling was called speculation.

To keep profits high, many workers were paid miserably low wages in the 1800s. Some of them grouped together to campaign for higher wages and better working conditions, forming trade unions. Sometimes unions withdrew their labour, striking as a part of their campaign. As a result, many companies were forced to improve conditions and pay fairer wages.

During the last 100 years, some countries, such as the Soviet Union (the former name for Russia and its neighbours) and China, tried to organise their economies in a new way. Communist governments aimed to give power over production back to the workers. They took companies out of private ownership and placed them under state control.

The market

Today, many countries operate a mixed economy. Most are run on the capitalist system, but many keep certain important services or industries under state control. A few countries call themselves communist, but even in these countries capitalist companies are now allowed to operate and there is a degree of private ownership. Industries controlled by the state are said to be nationalised. If they are returned to private ownership, they are privatised. Since the 1980s, many industries have been privatised around the world.

The world economy is increasingly organised on global rather than national lines. Transnational firms operate in their own interest rather than that of any single nation. Some giant corporations are richer and more powerful than individual countries. International treaties and organisations, such as the World Trade Organization (WTO), lay down rules about how countries should compete with each other.

If governments become unable to control or influence the companies operating within their borders, there is grave danger to democracy, since the main forces that shape the everyday lives of their citizens cannot be held to account.

In recent years, meetings of the World Trade Organization have been marked by demonstrations and protests against global capitalism.

One nation's economy

The United Kingdom is one of the world's richer countries. Its currency is called the pound sterling (£). The workforce makes up 49% of the total population.

If the workforce makes up 49% of the total UK population, what groups make up the remaining 51%?

The UK is rich in coal and was the first country in the world to go through an Industrial Revolution. Today, however, its mining and heavy industries have declined. The most valuable natural resources are oil and natural gas, which are produced offshore in Scottish waters. Over 27% of the workforce is employed in industry.

What products can you name that are made in factories in the UK?

Farming and fishing have been major UK industries in the past. Both are now strictly regulated by EU legislation. Farming employs far fewer people than 50 years ago, just 2% of the workforce. A quarter of the land area is given over to crop production. Fears that overfishing will destroy stocks of fish have led to strict quotas being imposed for catches.

The City of London is one of Europe's major centres of banking, finance, insurance and trading in stocks and shares.

Can you find out:
- Which manufacturing firm employs the largest number of people in your region/city? What does it make?
- Are the company's headquarters in this country or in another?
- How many people does the company employ? What percentage are men and what percentage are women? Are some of them part-time? Has the number increased or decreased over the last few years?
- Does the company have to import raw materials to make its products? Where do they come from?
- Which trade unions represent workers in the company?
- Where does the company sell its goods?

Services such as tourism, catering, shops, insurance or e-commerce now employ about 71% of the workforce. London's City district is a world centre of finance and banking.

Bread-and-butter issues

Companies provide work for people, and the wages paid to workers are in turn used to buy other goods and keep the economy running. All kinds of factors affect the economy. They include wage levels, transport and distribution costs, price levels, the rates of interest for savers and borrowers, and the buying and selling of shares in companies.

Foreign exchange rates can dictate whether exports and imports are profitable or costly. The European Union operates a single market and many of its members are now phasing in a single currency, the Euro.

Governments want to prevent inflation, or prices, running out of control. At the same time, they don't want the economy to stand still. It is a difficult balancing act between the two. If workers are sacked, it may make a firm more profitable, but it will also mean that there are fewer people able to buy goods, new houses or cars.

The degree to which the economy is managed by the government varies according to its political agenda. There are many different economic theories. A government may influence the economy in various ways, for example by passing laws, by printing money, by controlling a central bank, by giving grants to certain industries or regions, by nationalising or privatising industries. A government's financial plans may be presented to the parliament in a regular budget.

Governments, whether national, regional or local, normally finance their activities with taxes. Taxes are payments that have to be made to the government by individual citizens, or by companies and other organisations. Taxes may be charged on goods at the point of sale. They may be charged on income, on money that has been inherited when someone dies, on property, or on the licensing of cars or televisions. According to some politicians, governments should keep taxes as low as possible. According to others, taxes should be kept high.

Nobody enjoys paying taxes, but taxation is at the heart of any discussion about citizenship, because without it society could not function. It is normally taxation that pays for roads, pensions, schools and ambulances. Citizens who try to get out of paying their taxes may think they think are just hurting the government, but in reality they are hurting old people, children, and even themselves.

What might be the advantages of the Euro? Why do some people think the UK should join, while others disagree?

List as many types of taxation as you can think of. Should governments always try to keep taxation low? Are there any situations when a good citizen should refuse to pay taxes?

In and out of work

Working conditions have changed greatly since the 1800s and early 1900s. Women now make up a far greater proportion of the workforce, although in most parts of the world they are still struggling to gain equal pay to men. Jobs once done by people can now be done by machines. The development of personal computers and the Internet has made it possible for many people to work from home instead of in big offices.

Governments in most countries set out the rules and conditions of employment. In many countries, for example, there are public holidays, minimum wages, limits on hours worked, and rights to time off for a worker who is ill or expecting a baby. Many governments provide payments or retraining for people who remain unemployed. Unemployment takes away from people their economic power and influence.

Do citizens have a responsibility to work in order to support themselves and their families? Do governments have a duty to make sure that there is enough work for everyone?

Surveyors check the lie of the land at a building site. It is up to governments, employers and trade unions to ensure that there are equal job opportunities for all.

Most businesses need both managers and a workforce. The ways in which they behave towards each other are called industrial relations. A contract of employment involves duties on both sides. The employer has the right to expect hard work and honesty, the employee has the right to fair treatment, personal safety, a secure job and a decent wage. Employers may band together in organisations to further their interests, while employees may join trade unions to help them achieve their rights.

Name some of the organisations set up by employers, and some major UK trade unions.

A fair deal for consumers?

The workforce produces food, goods and services. Who buys them? We all do. We consume them (use them up). More and more money is spent on advertising and marketing goods, to persuade the public to buy things. In the last 40 years or so, many citizens have begun to see themselves as consumers and to demand that the products they buy are safe, well-made and sold at a fair price.

Do advertisements always tell the truth? What should consumers expect in terms of food labelling? What rights do you have when you buy something?

Rich world, poor world

If, as the song says, 'money makes the world go round', parts of the planet must be travelling at different speeds. News reports often describe some countries as 'poor' and some as 'rich'. What exactly does this mean?

National wealth can be measured in many ways. For example, what is the average income per citizen in one year? What is the GDP (gross domestic product) – the value of all the goods and services produced, foreign-owned or not, within national borders over one year? What is the GNP (gross national product) – the value of all nationally owned goods and services, abroad or at home, over one year?

In 1997 the GNP per head for the UK was US$20,870. Can you find out the figures for:
• Brazil
• Canada
• Ethiopia
• Germany
• India
• Irish Republic?

What makes one country rich and another poor? It is not the willingness of its citizens to work hard. In fact the poorer a country, the harder its people often have to work. A country may be poor if it has dry desert rather than rich farmland, if it suffers from frequent droughts or hurricanes, if it has no oil or gold or other minerals, or if it is located far from any sea or river ports.

Children at a village school in Mali, Africa. Mali is a very poor country bordering the Sahara, but its people are eager for education and progress.

A country will also remain poor if another country takes away its wealth, as happened during the 1800s and 1900s in Africa, when its lands were mostly ruled as colonies of powerful European countries. Now independent, African nations are among those that have borrowed money from the richer countries in order to survive. But the interest they have to pay on these debts makes it impossible to provide adequate education, start up new industries

or develop new sources of power. They are caught in a trap. Many people argue that the richer countries should cancel the debts. Others believe all debts should be paid as a matter of principle.

What do you think about 'international debt'? Find some media examples of discussion about world debt and foreign aid.

Many poor countries depend on aid being sent to them by the wealthier parts of the world. This may take the form of food, money for investment, or the building of dams or hospitals. The aid is necessary and welcome, but most people now agree that the best kind of international aid helps people to help themselves – by assistance with education or training, for example. Too many rich countries attach 'strings' to aid deals – promising aid, for example, only if the poorer country accepts a military base on their territory or uses equipment made in the rich country to carry out the work for which the aid is being given. Sales of arms (which promote employment in the rich country) may give power to repressive regimes in poor countries. Use of dam-building machinery (made in the rich country) to provide water in an arid, underdeveloped area may lead to large-scale irrigation projects, when small-scale well-drilling would be better suited to local needs.

Citizens, work and money

It has been said that we don't live in order to work, we work in order to live. Being a good citizen means understanding the economic system. It means knowing about work and lack of work, about working hard and making a success of things. It means helping to bring about good working practices, fairness in the workplace, and equal opportunities for all.

Citizens should find out what use money is put to while it sits in the bank. They should think about how they use their money, where they invest it and whom it benefits. They should find out if advertisements tell the truth and remain watchful as consumers. They should think globally. If one half of the world is profiting at the expense of the other half, the whole system remains in danger of collapse.

Politics influences how the society in which we live is structured, organised and administered. Society can be changed through political processes and action. Political processes affect many aspects of our lives including what we learn at school, the price of goods in the shops, payment for medicines and health care, and many other things.

Some big ideas

Many kinds of political system have developed over the ages. There have been tribes in which there is little organisation beyond the family group or the clan, and others where power has been held by a chief. In these societies, little is expected from a citizen except loyalty to the group. In return the group protects and nurtures the individual.

Name some constitutional monarchies that exist today.

There have been monarchies and empires, some of which still exist. They are ruled by kings, queens, princes or emperors. Normally, rule is passed down from father or mother to son or daughter, although at times rulers have been elected by other princes or nobles. Monarchs used to have complete power over their subjects, but today most are constitutional monarchs – rulers whose powers are limited by laws passed by their subjects.

Through history, there are many examples of tyrants and dictators – soldiers or other individuals who seize power by force and who rule by personal decree rather than by law. In most dictatorships, the citizen has very few rights, or none at all. In the 20th century, many dictators followed a form of politics called fascism, which started in Italy in the 1920s. Fascists believe that the citizens have few individual rights, only a duty to serve the nation. They are opposed to democracy.

Can you name any countries under military government today?

Benito Mussolini (1884-1945) founded the Fascist movement in Italy in 1921. Fascism took its name from the fasces, *a bundle of sticks containing an axe, which was the symbol of state power in Ancient Rome. Mussolini abolished democratic rule in Italy and adopted extreme, aggressive, nationalist policies. Fascism was supported by some British people in the 1930s and still attracts followers today.*

The word republic comes from the Latin language, used by the Ancient Romans. *Res publica* meant 'the public matter' – that is, the state. Rome became a republic in 509BC, when its people threw out the kings who ruled them. Today, a republic usually means a country with a head of state, normally a president, who has been elected or appointed with public approval.

Name some countries that currently have the status of republic.

Republics give power to the citizens, so they are closely linked with the idea of democracy. Democracy grew up over 2500 years ago in a city state called Athens, which was part of Ancient Greece. It meant rule by the people – that is, by a public assembly. That is still true today, with the assemblies taking the form of parliaments, senates, councils and many other public gatherings. The ancient idea of democracy was not based upon the equality of all citizens, but only on the equality of important people in society. The ideal of equality for everyone did not really become widespread until the 1700s, and it was only in the last 100 years that most of today's democracies gave the vote to all citizens – including women, poor people and minorities.

In recent times, many different kinds of government have claimed to be democracies. Communists put forward the idea that in a society suffering from economic injustice, true democracy means the seizing of power and rule by the working class, through the Communist Party that represented it. However, some leaders, such as the Georgian Joseph Stalin (1879-1953), used the Communist Party as a means to take on the personal powers of a dictator, murdering and imprisoning anyone who disagreed with them.

Anarchists mostly believe that true democracy is not about government but about cooperation and agreements between individuals and voluntary organisations, such as trade unions. They oppose any notion of citizenship that relates to the state.

Governments of the so-called 'Western' countries – such as those of Western Europe, North America, Australia, New Zealand – believe that that the fairest democratic system is a multi-party or pluralist system. Political parties can be formed by anybody, to campaign about important issues. The parties put up members to stand for election to an assembly. If they receive enough support, they are voted in by the public. As well as general elections and local elections, there might be referendums or plebiscites to vote upon particular policies or issues.

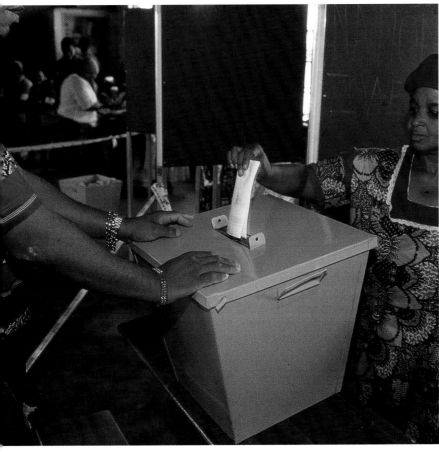

What examples can you give of a referendum being held, or the possibility of one being held in the future?

In 1994, for the first time in its history, South Africa held democratic elections which included all its citizens. Seven political parties were elected to the National Assembly. The African National Congress (ANC) won the most seats and so formed the government.

How is the House of Lords made up? What reforms to the House of Lords are being discussed?

In the last 10 years, more and more countries around the world have taken up pluralist systems of government. However, pure democracy is a hard ideal to achieve. In some countries, such as the United States, only political parties that can raise large amounts of funds, such as the Republicans and the Democrats, stand a real chance of being elected. In the United Kingdom, one part of the government, called the House of Lords, is not elected, so it could be argued that the UK is only a partial democracy. In many countries certain parties are banned from taking part in elections – often on the grounds that they are anti-democratic.

Should parties who wish to abolish democracy be allowed to take part in a democratic election?

Party politics

Political parties may be formed to campaign on a single issue – such as the environment – or to put forward a more general political theory and plan of action based on shared ideas – an ideology. By forming a party, people who share the same ideology can organise a campaign and perhaps gain power. Their plans

How many political parties can you think of which are active in UK elections (in general elections, Welsh Assembly or Scottish Parliament elections, or in EU elections)? The big parties are well known, but there are many smaller ones who put up candidates from time to time. Find out about some of the following parties and what they stand for. To what extent do you agree with their point of view?

British National Party
Communist Party
Conservative and Unionist Party
Democratic Labour
Democratic Left
Democratic Unionist Party
Green Party
Labour Party
Liberal Democrats
Marxist Party
Mebyon Kernow
Natural Law Party
Official Monster Raving Loony Party
Plaid Cymru/The Party of Wales
Scottish National Party
Sinn Fein
Social Democratic and Labour Party
Socialist Labour Party
Socialist Workers' Party
UK Independence Party
Ulster Unionist Party

may be written out and explained to the electorate in a detailed statement called a manifesto. They may be promoted in a radio or television broadcast.

A party's name often reflects its political viewpoint. However, this is not always so, and it is common for people to describe political parties as 'right-wing', 'left-wing' or 'centre'. These phrases go back a long way – they have their origins in the seating plan of the National Assembly during the French Revolution (1789-99). They are a useful shorthand, but these descriptions tend to be very subjective, based on the individual's point of view of what is 'normal'.

Racist or fascist groups are sometimes referred to as the 'extreme right'. Right-wing groups are generally seen as being in favour of traditional values and opposed to change or reform. Conservatives generally support free-market capitalism, private ownership and low taxation. Many conservatives in other European countries call themselves Christian Democrats.

Liberal means 'supporting progressive political reform'. Social democrats also see themselves as progressive. Both support a capitalist economic system, but place an emphasis on social justice and welfare. Parties using these names would normally be seen as belonging to the centre.

Freedom of speech is an important part of any democracy. Here, a campaigner addresses the crowd at Speakers' Corner in Hyde Park, London. Find out about laws which restrict or promote freedom of speech and expression in the UK.

Invite a locally elected politician to your school to discuss the make-up of the local council, the Welsh Assembly, Scottish Parliament or UK Parliament. Find out the party membership of the elected representative. Why might some candidates stand as independent - not members of any political party?

The left wing traditionally takes in socialists and communists, who may support public ownership, nationalisation and controlled economies rather than 'free' markets.

Some political language doesn't fit very easily into a simple left-right view of the world. *Green* means 'campaigning on environmental issues'. *Nationalist* may refer to the values of the extreme right, but may also refer to any centre or left-wing party that supports self-rule, majority rule or independence. *Radical* means 'going to the root of the matter' and means supporting drastic or fundamental change, left or right. *Militant* means viewing political activity as a combat or struggle.

Going to vote

In the UK, a general election to the UK Parliament must be held at least every five years. The world's biggest democracy is India, with 620 million people entitled to vote. There may be as many as 14,000 candidates and over 175 parties taking part! In most countries citizens have the right not to vote, but in some, such as Australia, citizens are required to vote by law.

Who is entitled to vote in UK elections? At what age do you think young people should be allowed to vote?

Suggest ways in which modern technology may alter the voting system.

In most elections around the world, the area being polled is divided into small areas called constituencies or wards. In each one there are polling stations. The way in which people normally vote is to go into a private booth and place a cross against the party or candidate of their choice on a sheet called the ballot paper. The voter then folds the paper and posts it into a box, which is taken to be counted once the poll has closed.

Representing the citizens

There are various ways in which votes can be turned into representation in an assembly or parliament. One way is for the

candidate who gets the most votes to be declared the winner and to represent that constituency in the parliament. This is sometimes called the 'first-past-the-post' system, because it is like a horse race in which there is only one winner. It is straightforward, easy to operate and depends strongly on the personality of the individual candidates. It is the method used in UK general elections.

Ballot papers are carefully counted by hand during a general election in the Irish Republic.

45

Critics of this system complain that it is unfair. The winning person may have 25,000 votes, while the person in second place may have 24,999. Don't all the people who voted for the person in second place also have the right to be represented? Likewise, some small political parties are never likely to poll enough votes to be represented in the first-past-the-post system.

One answer to this is proportional representation (PR), which takes into account the total number of votes for all parties, and allocates seats in proportion to the number of votes cast. Part of the vote for the Scottish Parliament and the Welsh Assembly is counted in this way. Critics of the PR system complain that it is too impersonal.

Sometimes, no single party gains enough seats to form a government or controlling group in an assembly. It is then normal for one or more parties to agree support for each other in a coalition. This allows them to achieve the backing they need to get things done.

Who needs politicians?

Today, many people say that they dislike politics and politicians. When an election is coming, they say, the politicians are always on television and in the newspapers making all kinds of promises. But when these people are elected, nothing really changes. "Why bother to vote?" "They're all the same."

In 1999, schoolchildren in the UK were asked what extra subjects they would like to study at school. They rated learning about personal relationships and money matters as far more important than studying politics. Thirty-four per cent showed no interest in

Why do you think many young people have so little interest in politics? What could make them more interested? How can young people make their views known and press for changes they support?

politics at all. What citizens all over the world dislike is political activity that produces few results, systems of government that do not meet their real needs or talk their language, a government that does not listen. Many politicians seem to be more interested in personal power than in representing the electorate. If a democratic system is not working properly, it can easily result in public apathy. If any government, democratic or otherwise, oppresses or ignores its own citizens, it may result in an explosion of public frustration.

For many years, men and women battled for the right to vote and to have a say in how decisions are made. That right should not be thrown away lightly, for it is precious. All citizens have a political role to play.

Can you think of any recent examples of riot or revolution against a government?

Non-party politics

Not all political action need be carried out by parties or directed through official assemblies such as parliaments and councils. Pressure groups are made up of individuals who get together to campaign about particular issues. These campaigns can cover all kinds of concerns, from the building of a road or airport to the closure of a factory or a school, protests about treatment of animals, or rights for disabled people. They may be protests about events in other countries or global issues such as pollution, sustainable development or world debt.

These demonstrators from the Greenpeace organisation are protesting against the planting of genetically modified crops.

47

Protests may be aimed at a particular company or organisation as much as against a government. Any such action is 'political', but the group may gain support from people who in other respects have very varying political views.

Input and output

For a society to function well, the input of the individual needs to be matched by the output of the political system. Each should empower the other in a two-way process, or partnership. This partnership may extend far beyond the mechanisms of government, such as voting or passing new laws. National, regional and local governments need to support initiatives put forward by individuals and voluntary groups in many areas of activity – for example, sports, health or community activities. Humans are very good at cooperation and partnership, as is often demonstrated in times of natural disaster or other crises. However this does not mean that governments should give up their basic responsibilities and say simply 'over to you'.

Name some formal groups of volunteers who work together to bring about particular improvements in society. Some will have concerns limited to the UK, others will have global concerns.

Getting things done

Getting things done is the purpose of all kinds of politics, official or unofficial. Utopias (ideal worlds) cannot be created. The world is in a state of constant change and does not allow the construction of a carefully designed house of cards. The wind will always blow the cards down. So is progress impossible?

About 150 years ago, the Victorians firmly believed that science, education and religion would bring about a brave new world at some time in the future. By 50 years ago, after two world wars, people were not so sure. Did human nature hold us back, always making the same old mistakes? Did history go round in circles?

Progress may jolt forwards rather than march steadily onwards, but it does take place. Who could deny that, for most citizens, things are better now than in the Middle Ages, when life was often short and brutal? The more comfortable lives led by many people today did not just happen – they were made to happen. Citizens thought up new ideas. More often than not, these collided head on with those of the people in power. The interaction between the two created a new situation, and that was challenged in its turn. It is this process, which still continues today, that gives us a way forward. As citizens, we all have a responsibility to do our part in working for a better world. We are each free to decide to do what our conscience tells us is right.

What would you say were five important ways in which modern society is better than life in the Middle Ages?

Who is the most important person in any country? Newspaper headlines might suggest that it is a queen or a king, a president or a prime minister. But in a democracy, you could argue that it is you! After all, citizens elect the governments and local councils to work for them, not the other way round.

Representing the nation

The head of state is the senior representative of his or her country. Some heads of states are kings and queens, while others are presidents. The head of state in the UK is Queen Elizabeth II. Many heads of state play only a symbolic part in running the country. The presidents of Ireland and Germany, for example, are important people who speak out on all kinds of issues, but they have little say in day-to-day government.

When did Queen Elizabeth II come to the throne? Who is the heir to the throne?

Queen Elizabeth II is a constitutional monarch. She rules the United Kingdom because her father did before her. Republicans believe that heads of state should be democratic representatives of their people.

In dealings with other countries, the head of state and the government as a whole are represented by appointed officials called ambassadors. These officials have special offices called embassies in foreign countries. Diplomats work internationally to improve relations between governments, promote trade and cultural links, and sort out any practical problems.

Running the country

Some heads of state, such as the presidents of the United States or France, do have the right to make the most important decisions – they have executive powers. They are normally selected in special presidential elections. In many countries, including the UK, the chief executive is the person named by the winning party in a general election. He or she is called a prime minister or premier. In the UK, the prime minister is formally invited by the monarch to form a government. Executive powers are shared by a group of people appointed by the prime minister, known as the cabinet. Cabinet members with responsibilities for special areas are called ministers or secretaries of state. The ministers in the cabinet are usually from the governing party or coalition, although not necessarily so.

Can you name the offices held by ministers in the cabinet with responsibility for particular aspects of government?

In a democracy, elected representatives include supporters of the government and people from any parties who disagree with the government, who make up the opposition. In many assemblies and parliaments, there is a chairperson, known as the speaker, who takes charge of the daily proceedings.

Which party is currently in power, and which is the main opposition party in the House of Commons (see page 52)? What is the name of the Speaker of the House of Commons? Which parties have a majority in the Scottish Parliament, and in the Welsh Assembly?

Collect newspaper cuttings about the changes in the House of Lords. Who do you think should be members of the second chamber? Should they be appointed by the House of Commons?

Representatives may sit in a single parliament such as the Swedish Riksdag, or in a parliament made up of two chambers. The United States Congress has two chambers – a Senate and a House of Representatives. The United Kingdom Parliament also has two chambers. They are made up of a directly elected House of Commons and a House of Lords (which is in the process of being reformed). The chief purpose of this second chamber will still be to approve or reconsider laws passed by the first chamber.

Rules of play

Every organisation, from a school to a football team, needs a set of rules so that everyone knows what can and can't be done. The rules of government, as well as any general principles on which the country is run, are normally drawn up in a group of special laws called the constitution. The United Kingdom is unusual in that it has no written constitution. Its constitution is simply the body of laws that have grown up in the country during its history. A government has various parts to play. They cover three main areas. First, its executive role is to work out policies, to take decisions, and to administer or run the country. Secondly, its legislative role is to pass any new laws that it thinks are needed. Thirdly, its judicial role is to make sure that existing laws are enforced and policed, and that criminals are brought to justice.

Passing new laws

Government policy is put into action by legislation, the making of new laws. The way in which this is done varies from one country to another.

Find out which bills are currently up before the UK Parliament. Choose one about which you have strong feelings. Write to your local MP and ask him or her to tell you their opinion of it. Find out the result of the debate and see how he or she voted.

In the UK, the process takes place in stages:

1) The government seeks advice from experts, lawyers or members of the public. It will then, with the help of the civil service, prepare draft legislation.

2) A document called a green paper is drawn up, which sets out the government's intentions.

3) When this has been discussed and debated, a revised white paper is published by the government.

4) A bill is presented to the House of Commons and debated in several stages. Any Member of Parliament may propose changes or amendments to the legislation, which are then voted on by all members present at the debate.

Find out about current examples of the House of Lords returning a bill to the House of Commons.

5) When the new bill has been passed by the UK House of Commons, it goes to the second chamber, the House of Lords, for debate and approval. The Lords may block the bill's progress, returning it to the Commons to be considered once again. The Commons, too, may seek to amend the legislation.

6) Finally, with the approval of both houses, the proposals become the law of the land.

The House of Commons is the most powerful chamber of the United Kingdom government.

Making government work

Government business is carried out by a large group of officials called civil servants. This is not a new idea – China had a civil service over 2000 years ago! A modern civil service advises the government and opposition on points of law or constitution and puts government policy into practice. It carries out the range of very important work that is necessary for society to function, from collecting taxes to checking on the safety of the food we eat. Civil servants work for the various government departments or ministries, each of which is normally headed by a member of the cabinet.

In some countries, such as the UK, the civil service is meant to be independent and non-political, working for whichever government party is elected. In other countries, such as the United States, large numbers of civil servants are appointed by an incoming government. That government and its officials are together called the administration.

Official business that is too slow or too complicated is sometimes referred to despairingly as 'red tape'. This term comes from the tape that was once used to bind up bundles of official or legal documents. To be effective, government business must be quick and to the point, yet still pay attention to detail. Even in the age of computers, complaints of too much 'red tape' are still common in most countries. Bureaucracy means 'rule by officials', and is often used sarcastically to describe the way in which civil servants or other officials seem to rule the lives of the public without being truly accountable.

Not all government business is carried out by civil servants. Particular jobs or public services may be hired out to private organisations or agencies. Special committees of experts, lawyers or other advisers may be paid to consider particular questions and to report back to the government. Bodies such as these often make many important decisions about the way we live. They are nicknamed quangoes (which is much easier to say than 'quasi-non-governmental organisations' in full!). They carry out all sorts of useful business, but sometimes come under criticism for having a lot of power without having been elected by the public.

A useful post was invented by Scandinavian governments in the 1950s. The ombudsman is a government official whose sole job is to investigate citizens' complaints against government departments or other public bodies. Many countries now appoint such officials.

Find out about the role of the ombudsman in the UK.

Welfare states

Many governments in the last hundred years have gone much further than just regulating the lives of their citizens. They have aimed actively to look after and protect citizens from hardship, poverty, poor health and lack of education. They have used public taxation to provide a welfare state.

In recent years, many Western countries have reduced social welfare. However, welfare states are still operated by most countries, to a greater or lesser degree. Typical welfare payments might include benefit for unemployment or disability, payments for the parents of small children, and old age pensions for senior citizens.

The UK National Health Service is funded by taxes and by National Insurance contributions. These are deducted from the salaries of working people.

Find out how much state pension is paid weekly to a senior citizen. Are there any other allowances to which they might be entitled? Work out roughly what their typical weekly expenses might be for:
• food
• domestic items, such as washing-up liquid
• heating
• electricity
• water
• telephone
• transport
• rent
• other.
How does their income compare with their expenditure?

In the UK, people visit Job Centres to seek work and register for unemployment benefit.

Most right-wing governments are suspicious of too much emphasis on state provision of welfare. They believe that generous payment of, say, unemployment benefit will put people off looking for work. They prefer the public to rely on private insurance or pension schemes rather than welfare. However, many centre and left-wing governments believe that the provision of welfare is a key role of good government, both as a basic principle of social justice and also as a practical way of running society. If unemployed people do not receive pay, they argue, they are more likely to commit crimes, or to become ill. So the state would probably end up paying out more in the end.

Should child benefit be given in equal amounts to every parent, or should poorer families receive a higher rate than richer families? How should the level of unemployment benefit be calculated? For how long should an unemployed person receive benefit?

Open government

In a democracy, citizens have a right to be kept informed, to see how their government makes decisions, and to know the truth behind the news. Citizens need to know who has real power and who is funding government and opposition political parties. For example, if a large transportation company makes donations to a government party, might that party change its policy on the taxation of roads and petrol? Being able to find out what is really going on is called transparency in government.

Governments that accept bribes or mislead the public are said to be corrupt. Many governments are not corrupt, but still do not keep the public fully informed. This may be because it is easier and quicker for them to carry out policy effectively without consulting the public all the time. It may be because they wish to avoid a public argument that might damage their political prospects. It may be that they assume citizens do not need or want to know.

Secrecy in government may take the form of laws to prevent information being made public. These are called official secrets. They include military or commercial information that could be of use to an enemy. They might also include information that a government wants to hide from its own citizens. In some countries, such as the United States, secrecy is balanced by freedom of information laws, which guarantee a citizen's right to know certain kinds of information.

Traditionally, the press questions government decisions on behalf of the public interest. Newspapers, books, radio and television – often referred to as communications media – play an important

Alistair Campbell, press secretary for the UK Prime Minister, Tony Blair, briefs journalists after the Labour victory in the 1997 general election.

part in passing on information as well as in asking important questions. Citizens may use the press to carry out this role, but they must also remember that the press itself may have an axe to grind – its own political or commercial motives.

Collect cuttings from three newspapers on the same day reporting on the same incident. Compare the angle taken, the language used, and the number of words written.

In many countries there is official or unofficial censorship of the media. This means that the government or some other body forbids certain news to be reported or certain opinions to be expressed. A free press is essential in any democracy.

Do you think that censorship should exist? What rules should be applied to keep some things out of the media? Should films be categorised as suitable for some age groups and not for others? If you were a parent, would you allow your children to watch any TV programme or video at any age?

Local government

In many ways, UK local government mirrors the operations of national or regional government. Councillors, often part-time, may represent political parties or stand independently. They debate and vote for policies at regular meetings of the council. The policy is carried out by a council staff acting as a kind of local civil service.

Them and us

Government is not always a very exciting notion. A lot of the work carried out by governments and councils often seems boring or is expressed in complicated legal language that sends even the politicians to sleep. Actually, the workings of government are fascinating – even if the government is a bad one! This is how human beings organise, how they get things done. This activity affects you every day, from the moment you get up in the morning to the moment you go to sleep.

Tell the politicians what you want. If they do not listen, spread the word. If they fail to deliver, tell them to go. Campaign and get involved. You'll soon find out that it's often much harder to get things done than you had imagined; that political and economic problems extend far beyond the ways in which parliaments do or don't work. But, as in most human activities, the quickest way of getting what you want is often to do it yourself.

What skills help people to be effective and politically active? Ask a local politician for his or her views. What methods could you use to spread information, or to campaign on an issue?

What happens when the will of an individual citizen or of some group or organisation conflicts with the will of society? Society, represented by the government, draws up rules to decide the outcome.

Can you imagine a world without rules or laws? It might sound like freedom – until you were robbed or attacked. Almost all societies that have ever existed have drawn up sets of laws. Their purpose may be to protect people or property from being harmed, to prevent conflict, to settle disputes, or to make society function more easily.

What rules does your school have and why do you think they exist? What rules or informal codes of behaviour make the classroom a good place to learn?

This figure representing Justice stands on top of the Old Bailey courts in London.

Fair play

If a non-democratic government passes laws, these laws may reflect public opinion, but they may not. In a dictatorship, laws may simply be decrees issued by the government. If a democratic government passes laws, they are meant to express the will of the majority of the people. However, that does not necessarily mean they are fair.

Think of examples of minorities who might feel that laws agreed by the majority were unfair to them. What might be done to achieve fairness?

For example, the majority of the people might pass laws which are unfair to a racial or religious minority. Fairness before the law is called equity.

Branches of the law

Just as we have various tiers of government, we have various tiers of law, at the international, national, regional and local level. Private or civil law deals with one-to-one disputes between individual citizens, groups or companies. Public law deals with issues in which the state is involved. It includes constitutional law (dealing with the principles of national government), administrative law (dealing with the practice of government), international law (dealing with agreements between different countries) and criminal law. Criminal law deals with cases such as murder, violence, fraud or theft, where the state prosecutes a suspected offender.

The two most widespread traditions of law in the world are known as Roman Law and Common Law. The first tradition developed from the laws of the Roman and Byzantine empires and came to be adopted in France, Germany, even as far away as Japan. The second tradition first developed in England. It was then adopted in Wales and Ireland, and later in the United States, Canada, Australia, New Zealand, India and many parts of Africa. In many countries, from Scotland to South Africa, the two traditions have become mingled.

The ruins of the ancient Forum in Rome. The Roman tradition of law has its origins in Ancient Rome. The Common Law tradition developed in medieval England.
Do you think modern law might be too wrapped up in history? Or does tradition and precedent mean that justice is thoroughly tried and tested?

Attend the public gallery of a courthouse near you while a judge is sitting.
- Did you think the proceedings were fair and just?
- Was there a jury, and did it seem to represent a fair cross-section of society?
- Does it make sense for a judge to wear special clothes or a wig?
- Did the court use language that people could easily understand?
- Did the accused seem to be intimidated?
- In your opinion, is there any way in which things could have been improved?

In the Roman tradition, the law is seen as a code of conduct and punishment, drawn up by the state. In the Common Law tradition, the law has always been based on precedent – the decisions made by judges over the centuries, case by case. Roman Law judges often investigate a crime, while common law judges act as 'referees' between lawyers representing the two sides.

Common Law has always placed great emphasis on a jury, a panel of ordinary citizens called in to decide whether a prisoner is guilty or not. The jury system is now used by both legal traditions, but only for more serious crimes.

Making laws work

Although governments are ultimately responsible for the judicial system, it is made to work on a day-to-day basis by a large number of public officials. In the front line are the police. Their job is to serve the community by assisting in emergencies, preventing crime, investigating crime, arresting people and charging them with breaking the law, and arranging for them to be brought to court.

Lawyers may be employed either by the state (the Public Prosecution Service) or by the individual citizen. In many countries there are different grades of lawyer, such as barristers and solicitors. In an English or Welsh criminal court, there will be lawyers acting for the prosecution and lawyers acting for the defendant. Each puts their case and may call witnesses to support their argument. Defendants have the right to present their own case, but they may not know the ins and outs of the system well enough to do this effectively in anything but the most clear-cut of situations.

The law draws the line between the wishes of the individual citizen and those of the state. When these conflict, it is the job of the police to enforce the law.

All cases come initially to a magistrates' court. If a magistrate decides that he or she does not have adequate sentencing powers to punish the defendant if found guilty, the case is passed on to a higher court where a judge will preside over the case. The judge considers the arguments and then sums up the legal position. If there is a jury, its members must consider the case and declare if they find the defendant guilty or not guilty. If guilty, the judge then decides the sentence.

Find out about how magistrates' courts work by inviting a Justice of the Peace (JP) or a court official to your school. Are JPs paid? How are they selected? What sentences can they give? How do they decide on an appropriate sentence?

Most judges in the United Kingdom are white, male and upper class, although this is beginning to change. Do you think the social background of the judge is relevant to the carrying out of justice?

Breaking the law

Laws vary greatly from one country to another. They reflect the culture and traditions of each society. Actions that are legal in one country may be illegal in another. In some countries drinking alcohol may always be illegal, in another the use of certain drugs. In some countries a man may take several wives, in another that would be forbidden. However, some laws are shared by all countries in the world. Crimes such as murder, theft and kidnapping are unacceptable to people everywhere.

A citizen's duty is to obey the law, but in return the judicial system has to consider why that law has been broken. Courts have to consider motive, social conditions and personal circumstances. In the event of a guilty verdict, these factors will influence the sentence given.

Is it ever right to break the law? Why do people break the law? List as many reasons as you can, giving an example in each case.

Penalties and punishments

The punishments used in a country make up its penal system. The system is designed to place limits on an offender's individual rights as a citizen by, for example, imposing a fine, or by depriving the offender of his or her liberty in jail.

In some countries the most serious offence is capital punishment – the death penalty. The death penalty has now been abolished by many countries, including the UK. It is still used in some countries, including China, Iran, Saudi Arabia and the United States. In 1998 executions were carried out in 36 countries around the world, and there were prisoners under sentence of death in 77 countries. Capital punishment is widely used as the penalty for murder, but in some countries it is also used for offences such as dealing in drugs.

Do you think that the death sentence is ever appropriate?

The electric chair is one of the execution methods used in the USA. Should a state have the right to kill its own citizens? Does capital punishment act as a deterrent to crime? It certainly does not allow for a reprieve, should new evidence cast doubt on the conviction.

In many countries, corporal punishment is a common penalty. This may range in severity from cutting off someone's hand to flogging or beating them. Less severe penalties include the payment of fines, payment of compensation or some form of community service.

What is the purpose of sending someone to prison? Is it simply punishment? Is it to deter others from committing crime? Is it to protect society from the offender? Is it to rehabilitate the prisoner, so that he or she can become a useful member of society?

Taking away the freedom of a citizen is a very common punishment. Prisons are normally run by the state, but in recent years private firms have been licensed to operate prisons in the United States and the UK. Conditions in prisons vary greatly across the world.

This is a punishment cell at Strangeways Prison, in England. Should prison conditions be harsh? If so, why? Is depriving a citizen of his or her liberty sufficient punishment, or should prison life itself be part of the penalty?

Citizens and the law

Law and punishment form a crucial part of the two-way contract between the citizen and society. A society which is unjust will not be able to maintain law and order.

Each citizen has a duty to understand and obey laws, but also has a right to expect laws to be passed democratically, to be just and carried out fairly. Police and prison officers deserve the public support of citizens, but they must fulfil their part of the bargain by being honest, even-handed and publicly accountable. The service of lawyers in court must be available to rich and poor alike, to guilty and not guilty, to educated and uneducated people, to minorities as well as majority groups. State funding of defence lawyers is called legal aid.

Find out about your local police force.
- What area does it cover?
- What is the purpose of the Police Authority and who are its members?
- How is it funded? How much does it spend in a year?
- How many people does it employ? Is it more or fewer than ten years ago?
- Is the local crime rate falling or rising for:
  - burglary?
  - violence against the person?
  - drugs offences?
- What percentage of the force is from ethnic minorities?
- What is the procedure for a citizen to make a complaint against the police?

Is there a single country in the world where every aspect of this social contract is honoured? All we can say with certainty is that some judicial and penal systems are much fairer than others, and that some are very unfair. The question then arises of how to make them better.

Find out who is entitled to legal aid.

Some would say the best way to improve things would be for each citizen not to break the law in the first place. In the real world, however, that is unlikely to happen. Citizens may campaign to change the judicial system. In a democracy, the political system should be the route through which change can be made. Campaigning may draw the attention of others, including those with political power, to the views of the campaigners and so assist the process of change.

Look for examples in the media of British citizens being in trouble with the law in other countries.

" It's not fair!" cries the child. "Life isn't meant to be fair!" replies the weary parent.

The principle of natural justice is much wider than the details laid out in laws and sets of rules. It is based upon the idea that there are certain values common to all human beings and which need to be recognised by one and all. This idea is shared by most religious beliefs, many philosophies and also by many political ideologies.

Chileans living in Britain demonstrate against the former Chilean dictator, Augusto Pinochet, in 1999. During Pinochet's rule in the 1970s, many of his opponents were tortured or killed.

Human rights...

From the 1700s onwards, many thinkers began to talk of human rights, declaring that – in the interests of common humanity – all citizens deserve to have certain basic needs met by society. Over the ages, this idea has been widely accepted and expanded to include many areas of human need. It has even been extended to take in the idea of animal rights.

DISAPPEAR

Examples of human rights include living in freedom rather than slavery, the right to have enough food, the right to receive healthcare and education, the right to work, the right to receive justice at the hands of the law, the right to vote, and the right to self-government. Freedom of speech is the right not to be censored, freedom of worship is the right to follow one's own religious beliefs, freedom of association is the right to organise political parties or trade unions. Equality of opportunity means giving every citizen equal chances, regardless of colour, gender or social background. In recent years, many people have become increasingly concerned about their right to privacy. Many human rights overlap and are linked with each other.

Rights are recognised and listed in many national constitutions, such as the United States Bill of Rights, and also in international charters such as the United Nations' Declaration of Human Rights. Charters often form the basis of legislation in member states, and are also often found in contracts of employment, or in the rule books of organisations.

If a company mistreats its employees, or dumps poisonous waste, it is possible to boycott its goods or take other forms of action. Countries that do not honour basic human rights or abuse their citizens often come under the criticism of other countries or of international watchdog organisations. They, too, may be forced to change their ways by political action such as trade embargoes.

The following excerpts come from the Universal Declaration of Human Rights, adopted by the United Nations in 1948.

Article 1: All humans are born free and equal in dignity and rights...

Article 2: Everyone is entitled to all the rights and freedoms set forth in this Declaration, without distinction of any kind, such as race, colour, sex, language, religion, politics or other opinion, national or social origin, property, birth or status.

Article 3: Everyone has the right to life, liberty and security of person.

Article 4: No one shall be held in slavery or servitude...

Article 5: No one shall be subjected to torture or cruel, inhuman or degrading treatment or punishment.

Many countries are all too eager to accuse others of abusing human rights, while turning a blind eye to injustices experienced by their own citizens. Many of the abuses officially abolished in the last 200 years still exist. In various parts of the world, citizens are still enslaved or tortured, women are treated as inferior beings, children are forced to work rather than go to school, people starve to death, and people are discriminated against because of their ethnic group or their religion.

A young girl at work in a carpet factory in Agra, India. In many parts of the world children are still made to work for a living.

Find out about the human rights record of the United Kingdom and compare it to those of other countries.

The honouring of human rights is not always straightforward, because some of those rights may conflict with others. Societies contain many different groups and it is hard to guarantee one citizen's freedom without treading on the toes of another.

Conflicts of interest have to be marked out by law. For example, it may be necessary to limit the right to free speech of racist citizens in order to allow other citizens the right to live free of fear and hatred. It may be necessary to limit the freedom to carry a gun (considered to be a right under the United States constitution) in order to protect other citizens from harm.

... and responsibilities

Outside a utopia, or ideal world, human rights are not absolute but conditional. In other words, it is generally believed that rights are matched by responsibilities and duties. If a state is to honour human rights within society and act democratically, then citizens (as individuals or as groups) should play a constructive part in society in return. Some political parties place greater emphasis on the citizen's duty to the state, others on the state's duty to its citizens. When governments call on citizens to perform duties, they might be seeking to escape their own responsibilities – and to save some money, too!

Where should the borders be drawn between the responsibility of the individual and that of the state or other authority? Supposing a village pond is full of rubbish. Should the villagers get together and clean it up? Or should that be the job of the local council? Find out about local Agenda 21 in your area.

In relation to the local community, the individual citizen clearly has a responsibility to avoid antisocial behaviour, such as driving too fast through the streets or making a neighbour's life a misery with loud noise or verbal abuse. Children are citizens, too. If a village provides them with a playground and swings, then their 'duty' to the community is to avoid smashing them. If they are provided with an education, it is their duty not to scare off other children from school by bullying.

A citizen's rights and duties go all the way from international, national and regional levels, down to community and family, couple or other social unit. The small picture is as important as the big picture. There is no virtue in talking about changing the world if you behave like a dictator in your own home.

Morals and ethics

At the end of this chain of rights and social responsibilities, meet the individual citizen. He or she has to decide for him or herself what seems right or wrong, and behave according to personal ideas of morality. It has been suggested that if each individual citizen behaved morally, there would be no need for prisons, laws or even government.

The trouble is, ideas of what is right or wrong vary greatly from one citizen to another. Systems of moral principles are called ethics. They may be based on religious belief, on cultural background, or simply on personal experience. Society is too diverse for simple solutions.

Firefighters place their own lives at risk in order to save the lives of other citizens.

For the good of all

List jobs in which people work to help others.

Individualism may be a force for good in society, but it may also bring about selfishness. In a world ruled by money, individualism may bring great material rewards. Even so, there are still many people who work to help their fellow human beings. For them, personal reward is often a less important motive than that of helping others.

Many national and international organisations have been founded in order to help others, save lives or protect human rights around the world. What can you find out about the work of the following? Add other organisations if you know of any that interest you particularly.

Amnesty International
Human Rights Watch
Médecins Sans Frontières (MSF)
Minority Rights Group International
International Red Cross/Red Crescent
Survival International
Voluntary Service Overseas (VSO)

This man has volunteered to work overseas, teaching mathematics at a school in Ghana.

73

Some people volunteer to help refugees or foster children who have no families. There are people who provide service to the community without being paid, such as providing food or transport for the elderly. In the UK, there are people who work for the Citizens' Advice Bureau, offering the public help with all kinds of practical everyday problems, such as bad debt, claiming benefit or consumer law.

What other types of voluntary activity do you know of?

Charities collect money for many good causes. They help raise funds for people with medical or social problems, they send money to relieve famine or earthquake victims, and they support campaigns against cruelty to animals. Acts of charity, or 'giving alms' as it was once called, are encouraged by most of the world's major religions. Many people who don't believe in God also support charitable behaviour.

Acts of charity show human kindness and cooperation at its best, but there is sometimes a danger in always seeing social problems in terms of charity. Giving money may relieve a particular problem, but it will not necessarily solve it. Indeed, it may just prolong the problem, allowing other parts of society or government to avoid their responsibility for dealing with it.

In the past, some scientists argued that human beings and other creatures developed or evolved slowly over the ages, and that it was the most aggressive ones that survived. Others have since pointed out that creatures which cooperate with each other stand an even better chance of survival. Humans have been successful on this planet because they are social animals. They often act in ways which balance their own interests and the welfare of others. They are capable of altruistic actions – behaving solely for the good of humanity in general or of other individuals.

Can you find out about the activities of some of the
following charity organisations? What do they do?
How do they raise money? How can they be helped?
Do you know any charities local to your own area?
Barnardos
Cancer Research Campaign
Children's Aid Direct
Help the Aged
National Trust
Oxfam
Royal National Lifeboat Institution (RNLI)
Royal Society for the Prevention of Cruelty to Animals
     (RSPCA)
Save the Children
Scope

*A lifeboat speeds to
the rescue of a ship in
trouble. In the United
Kingdom, the RNLI
collects funds as a charity
and relies on volunteers
to crew its lifeboats.*

Being a good citizen isn't about being a 'goody-goody' or a 'nerd'. It is about saying "Here I am, here's everybody else, let's get our act together, let's make things work." It's about making the world – including your own little corner of it – a good place to live.

Action stations

As individual citizens, we have little power. By joining forces with others, we have more chance of being effective. Being a good citizen means taking action. Try to find out what is going on in your community and in the wider world.

One key to active citizenship is communication. Argue your point by writing in to the newspapers, phoning in to the radio, collecting petitions. Take part. The Internet offers a great opportunity for citizens around the world to inform themselves and to communicate with each other. To campaign effectively, you must be organised. Before you hold a meeting, decide what is to be discussed. Draw up an agenda of items to be debated and make sure that ideas are clearly proposed to the meeting – in debating terms, in the form of a motion – and then voted on. That's democracy. At the end of the meeting, decide the best way of moving forwards and taking further steps.

Of course, people can be active citizens in many different ways. Not everyone is the type to complain or campaign and organise. Good citizens can quietly get on with helping their family or their neighbours. Find out the best way in which you can help people in your community. Speak out against bullying in school. Learn first aid. Start up a youth club or a football club. Organise a carnival. Get people talking to each other.

It is often said that in the old days people were more neighbourly, that crime was less common – that people generally were better citizens. A lot of such talk may be wishful thinking. About 150 years ago, in the Victorian period, there was much talk of public morality and the virtue of hard work. However, in reality that age was plagued by social injustice, crime and hypocrisy.

It is true that in the last hundred years many traditional societies have been disrupted. The pace of life has become faster, the pressures have increased. Families no longer always live in the same neighbourhood as their relatives. Many people stay indoors, watch television a lot and become isolated. Many of the links between different parts of society have become severed. If you do send messages around the world on the Internet, don't forget to say good morning to your next-door neighbour, too.

Children take part in a demonstration about cruelty in pig-farming.

77

Society is a bit like the human nervous system – the brain and nerves that keep a human body alive. Signals rush from all parts of the body to the brain and back again, telling different parts of the body how to behave and how to react. They protect the body by making it aware of pain, making it aware of pleasure, keeping it moving. Bursts of electric energy called pulses surge along the nerves and leap across the gaps between them.

In society, individual citizens are like the nerves, sending communications to other members of society, to the family, neighbours or the government. Like nerves, citizens protect the body as a whole, they warn of danger and keep it moving. They work together to get things done.

"Never doubt that a small group of thoughtful, committed citizens can change the world. Indeed, it is the only thing that ever has."

Margaret Mead (1901-78)

How are members of your class or year group involved as volunteers to work for a better society? Is there any project with which you yourself could become involved? Keep a diary to record any personal voluntary involvement such as:

- sponsored walks
- fund-raising
- canvassing
- social work, such as visiting elderly people
- babysitting
- environmental work.

Some Useful Websites

Charity/action

Barnardos	http://www.barnardos.org/
Charity Commission England & Wales	http://www.charity-commission.gov.uk/
Children's Aid Direct	http://www.cad.org.uk/
Help the Aged	http://www.helptheaged.org.uk/
RNIB	http://www.rnib.org.uk/
RNLI	http://www.rnli.org.uk/
RSPCA	http://www.rspca.org.uk/
Samaritans	http://www.samaritans.org.uk/
Scope	http://www.scope.org.uk/

Communications media

BBC	http://www.bbc.co.uk/
The Glasgow Herald	http://www.theherald.co.uk/
The Guardian	http://www.guardian.co.uk/
Internet Mailing list directory	http://www.liszt.com/
ITN	http://www.itn.co.uk/
The Times	http://www.the-times.co.uk/

Economics

Confederation of British Industry	http://www.cbi.org.uk/
Consumers' Association	http://www.which.net/
The Economist	http://www.economist.com/
Trades Union Congress	http://www.tuc.org.uk/

Education

Channel 4	http://www.4learning.co.uk/
Education (BBC)	http://www.bbc.co.uk/education/home/
Education (British Council)	http://www.britcoun.org/education/index.htm

Environment

Conservation International	http://www.conservation.org/
Countryside Commission	http://www.countryside.gov.uk/
Environment Agency	http://www.environment-agency.gov.uk/
Friends of the Earth	http://www.foe.co.uk/
Greenpeace	http://www.greenpeace.org/
UN Earthwatch	http://www.unep.ch/earthw.html
World Conservation Union	http://www.iucn.org/
Worldwide Fund for Nature	http://www.panda.org/

Government

UK Parliament	http://www.parliament.uk/
Bills before UK Parliament	http://www.parliament.the-stationery-office.co.uk/
Scottish Parliament	http://www.ScottishParliament.co.uk/
Welsh Assembly	http://www.wales.org.uk/

Human rights

Amnesty International	http://www.amnesty.org/
Child Rights	http://www.crin.org/
Human Rights Watch	http://www.hrw.org/

International action and aid

Concern Worldwide	http://www.irishnet.com/concern.htm
International Committee of the Red Cross	http://www.icrc.org/
Médecins Sans Frontières	http://www.msf.org/
Oxfam	http://www.oxfam.org.uk/
Panos Institute	http://www.oneworld.org/panos
Poverty: information	http://www.undp.org/toppages/ poverty/povframe.htm
Refugee Council	http://www.refugeecouncil.org.uk/
Save the Children	http://savethechildren.org.uk/
Survival International	http://www.survival-international.org.uk/
Voluntary Service Overseas	http://www.vso.org.uk/

International affairs

Association of Caribbean States	http://www.acs-aec.org/
Association of SE Asian Nations	http://www.asean.or.id/
Commonwealth of Nations	http://www.thecommonwealth.org/
Council of Europe	http://www.coe.fr/
European Union	http://www.europa.eu.int/
NATO	http://www.nato.int/
Organization of American States	http://www.oas.org/
United Nations	http://www.un.org/
UN Development Programme	http://www.undp.org/
UNESCO	http://www.unesco.org/
UN High Commissioner for Refugees	http://www.unhcr.ch/
UNICEF	http://www.unicef.org/

Political parties

Conservative Party	http://www.conservative-party.org.uk/
Labour Party	http://www.labour.org.uk/
Liberal Democrats	http://www.libdems.org.uk/
Plaid Cymru	http://www.plaidcymru.org.uk/
Scottish National Party	http://www.snp.org.uk/
SDLP	http://www.sdlp.ie/
Sinn Féin	http://sinnfein.ie/
Ulster Unionist Party	http://www.uup.org/

Religious and other beliefs

Atheism	http://www.hti.net/www/atheism
British Humanist Association	http://www.humanism.org.uk/
Buddhism	http://www.ciolek.com/WWWVL-Buddhism.html
Catholic Information Service	http://www.cin.org/
Church of England	http://www.church-of-england.org/
Church of Scotland	http://www.churchofscotland.org.uk
Church in Wales	http://www.churchinwales.org.uk
Hinduism	http://hinduismtoday.kauai.hi.us/ashram
Islam	http://www.unn.ac.uk/societies/ islamic
Judaism	http://www.jewfaq.org/
Sikhism	http://www.sikhs.org/
Statistics, religious	http://adherents.com/

Social issues

Anti-Racist Alliance	http://www.blacknet.co.uk/youthara
Citizens' Advice Bureau	http://www.nacab.org.uk/
Commission for Racial Equality	http://www.cre.gov.uk/
Health Education Board (Scotland)	http://www.hebs.scot.nhs.uk/
National Health Service UK	http://www.nhs50.nhs.uk/
Police UK	http://www.police.uk/

Statistics and information

Flags	http://www.flags.ndirect.co.uk/
Government information UK	http://www.open.gov.uk/
Language statistics	http://www.sil.org/Ethnologue/
Population Concern	http://www.prb.org/
State of the World: Indicators	http://www.igc.apc.org/
UK statistics	http://www.statistics.gov.uk/

agenda A list of things to be done or ideas to be discussed.

agnostic Someone who believes that humans cannot know whether there is a God, or have faith in anything other than their own experience.

aid Food, resources or money sent from one country to help another.

altruistic Expecting no reward.

ambassador An official representing his or her country internationally.

anarchist Someone who opposes all idea of nation states or government.

animal rights The basic need for proper and humane treatment of animals.

antisocial Against the interests of the community or society.

assembly A public gathering of people, especially a parliament.

asylum A place of refuge, or the legal right to stay in a foreign country to which one has had to flee.

atheist Someone who does not believe in the existence of a God or of gods.

ballot paper The slip of paper used for casting votes in an election.

barrister In the UK and some other countries, a lawyer entitled to appear in courts at all levels.

benefit A payment or award within a welfare state.

boycott To refuse to buy certain goods or services, or to refuse certain actions as a protest.

cabinet The senior members of a government, responsible for administration.

candidate Somebody putting themselves forward for a job appointment or an election.

capitalist (1) Someone who makes a living by selling stocks and shares. (2) Someone who supports a free market rather than a controlled economy.

capital punishment Carrying out a death sentence, legal execution.

censorship The restriction or prevention of communication.

census An official count of the population.

centralised Organised around a central point or a single place.

chamber One division of a parliament or other assembly, such as the UK House of Commons.

charity (1) Love of one's fellow human beings. (2) An organisation whose aim is to help other people.

citizen The individual as a member of society or a nation.

citizenship Acting as a good citizen within society.

city state An independent state based upon a single city rather than a whole country.

civil law The branch of law which deals with private matters and disputes between individuals.

civil rights The rights of the citizen within society, such as voting or equality of opportunity.

civil servant A state-employed official who carries through government business.

clan A traditional social grouping made up of people who are descended from the same ancestor.

coalition A union of various political parties to form a single government.

Common Law A tradition of law that originated in England.

communist (1) Believing that most property and resources should be shared or publicly owned. (2) Believing that workers, or a party representing the workers, should be in charge of production and manufacture. (3) Believing that a single party representing the workers should control all political and economic activity in a state.

community (1) The part of society in which a citizen lives, such as a village or a suburb. (2) A part of society which shares a common interest or background.

community service Helping people in the community, either as a volunteer or as part of a punishment.

compensation Paying someone back for something, making up for an injury.

conservative (1) In favour of tradition, cautious. (2) Believing in the free market and private ownership of property and resources.

constituency An area represented in parliament.

constitution The laws, rules and principles by which a country is governed.

constitutional monarch A king or queen whose powers have been limited by democratic reform.

consume To use up, eat or buy.

continent One of the major geographical divisions of the world – Europe, Asia, North or South America, Africa, Oceania or Antarctica.

corporal punishment Punishing someone physically, as with a beating.

criminal law The branch of the law which deals with crime.

currency The form of money used within a country or a region.

defendant Somebody accused in a court of law.

democracy Rule by the people, or by their elected representatives.

dependency Any territory or land ruled by another nation.

devolve To transfer or pass on responsibility, duty or power. The UK government has devolved some power to Scotland, Wales and Northern Ireland.

dialect A non-standard form of language, as spoken by people from a certain social class or region. It may have its own words, accent and structure.

dictator An unelected ruler with absolute power.

diplomat Someone who represents their government abroad.

distribute To send goods, produce or information out to various places.

economic To do with money, labour, producing or consuming goods.

election Choosing people to be members of an organisation or a government.

electorate The people entitled to vote.

embassy An office representing one country's government in another country.

empire A group of countries or territories ruled by a single government.

enfranchise To give someone the vote.

equity Fairness before the law, common sense, even-handedness.

established Of a church, official or nationally recognised

ethics Ideas of morality, of what is right or wrong.

ethnic group A group of people sharing common descent, culture or language.

executive Having the power to decide on a course of action.

export To sell goods to another country.

fascism A political belief in a powerful centralised state, aggressive nationalism or racism.

federal Forming a union of self-governing units.

first-past-the-post An election won by whoever gains the most votes.

foreign affairs Matters affecting the relations between countries.

foreign exchange Exchanging the currency of one country for that of another.

freedom of information The legal right of the public to find out information.

free market Economic activity which is not controlled or limited by government.

free press The ability of the press to report news and ideas without interference or censorship.

generation All the people born in the same period, an age group.

government (1) The body of people that runs a country. (2) The way in which a country is run.

green (1) Friendly to the environment. (2) Campaigning on environmental issues.

gross domestic product (GDP) A measure of the wealth of a nation. It may be based on various calculations. One is the total of selling prices, less the cost of bought-in materials. Another is the national total of wages, rents, dividends, interests and profits. A third, and the one most commonly used, is the national spending on goods and services.

gross national product (GNP) A measure of the wealth of a nation. It is calculated in much the same way as GDP, but includes the profits that residents in the country have made overseas.

hierarchy Any society or organisation that is graded in order of rank.

home affairs An area of government responsibility including law and order. Sometimes called interior affairs.

human rights The basic need for justice and equality, which every human deserves.

humanist Someone who bases his or her philosophy on human needs and interests rather than on religious teachings or scripture.

ideal An idea of something in its best possible form.

ideology A system of ideas, a theory.

import To buy goods from another country.

independent Of a country, self-governing, free of foreign rule.

industrial relations The way in which employers and employees treat each other.

industrial revolution The rapid growth of technology and manufacture in the 1700s and 1800s.

inflation A rise in the cost of living.

interdependent Relying on each other.

interest A sum of money paid by a bank to an investor or owed by a debtor to a creditor.

jingoism Excessive patriotism.

judicial To do with law and order.

jury A panel of citizens selected to decide upon guilt in a court case.

law A government-made rule which people have to obey.

legal aid Legal fees paid by the state.

legislative Making new laws (legislation).

liberal (1) Broad-minded, supporting freedom. (2) Supporting a centre view of politics with a mixed economy.

magistrate An official who judges cases in lower courts of law.

majority The largest number within a group of people or a country.

manifesto A public statement outlining a political plan of action.

mayor The leading official within a city, town or local government.

media Methods of communication, such as newspapers, magazines, radio and television.

militant Combative.

military (1) To do with the armed forces. (2) The armed forces.

minister One of the senior government members, responsible for an area of administration.

minority One of the smaller groups of people within a group of people or a country.

mixed economy An economy which takes in both public and private ownership.

monarchy A country ruled by a king or a queen.

morality An understanding of right and wrong.

motive The reason someone might have for doing something, such as committing a crime.

multinational Based in many countries. Also transnational.

nation (1) A country that is internationally recognised as an independent state. (2) More generally, a country and all the people who live in it.

nationalise To turn private companies over to state control.

nationalist (1) Supporting the creation of an independent or liberated nation. (2) Believing in the superiority of one's own nation.

nation state A country seen as a unit of government.

official secret Information which by law may not be released to the public.

ombudsman An official appointed to investigate public complaints about government and the civil service.

opposition The members of parliament or some other democratic assembly who oppose the government.

patriotism Love of one's country.

penal system The system of sentencing and punishing offenders.

pension A sum of money paid to people who have retired from work. Companies may pay pensions to former employees, and governments may pay a state pension to senior citizens.

plebiscite or referendum A public vote held to decide upon a particular issue.

pluralist Made up of several political parties.

political To do with the way in which society is organised, with government and change.

poll To find out public opinion, to take a vote on something.

polling station A place where people go to vote during an election.

precedent A previous ruling, taken as guidance for a legal judgement.

pressure group A group of people formed to campaign on a particular issue.

prime minister A head of government who is not also head of state. Also, premier.

principle A guiding rule of belief or conduct.

privatise To return state-owned enterprises to private control.

proportional representation A system of election in which all the votes cast go towards deciding the final result.

prosecute To take somebody to court and make the case against them.

quango A non-elected body appointed by the government.

quota Permitted amounts, numbers or proportions.

racism Believing that humanity can be divided into groups called races, and that some races are superior to others.

radical Going to the root of the matter, extreme, basic.

raw materials The basic materials needed to manufacture something. Cotton fibre is a raw material used by the textile industry.

referendum A vote held to decide a particular political issue rather than to elect a government.

refugee Somebody who flees from one country to another as a result of persecution or poverty.

republic A country with an elected head of state and government.

Roman Law A legal tradition that began in the Roman and Byzantine empires.

secular Non-religious.

sentence The punishment decided upon by a court of law.

share A certificate of money invested in a company, as a form of part-ownership.

socialist Supporting public ownership of property and resources.

society The whole community, people in general.

solicitor In the UK and some other countries, a lawyer who appears at lower courts, offers legal advice and prepares cases for barristers.

speaker The person who chairs proceedings in a parliament or assembly.

speculation Trading on the price of company shares, hoping to make a profit as they rise and fall.

status quo The existing situation.

strike To stop working, in order to force employers to change working conditions.

subject A citizen living in a monarchy.

subjective Depending upon the viewpoint of the individual.

tax Payments made to the government in order to fund public services and other activities.

theocracy A state ruled or controlled by religious leaders.

trade embargo A ban on trade imposed by one country against another.

trade union An association of workers formed to campaign for better wages and working conditions.

treasury The department of government responsible for budgets and economic policy.

treaty An official agreement between nations.

tyrant (1) A ruler who has absolute power. (2) An oppressive or unjust ruler.

undemocratic Not allowing the public to choose or speak out.

utopia An ideal or imaginary world.

veto The right to prevent or forbid a policy or course of action.

volunteer Someone who offers to do something for no personal reward.

vote Indicating your choice in an election or a debate.

watchdog An organisation set up to monitor services or actions.

welfare Money or other benefits provided by the government to help the needy.

welfare state A government which sets out to protect and provide for its citizens.

witness Somebody who is called into a court of law to give information relevant to the case being tried.

Index